MYST S
OF THE AN L D

WHO WERE THE DRUIDS?

A. P. FITZPATRICK

CASSELL PLC

WEIDENFELD & NICOLSON
LONDON

The Druids. The name conjures up many images; white-robed believers at the summer solstice at Stonehenge, mistletoe, a cartoon character. All are images inspired by the ancient Druids, but who were they?

To try and solve this mystery we must look at evidence, archaeological and historical, which is 2,000 years old and dates back to the Iron Age. We shall see that the modern images of Druids are only a few hundred years old and, although they may now seem comic, they symbolize some of the first serious western attempts to understand the antiquity of humanity.

A romantic 1815 acquatint of 'an Arch Druid in his Judicial Habit'. The artefacts shown are either hundreds of years earlier than the first evidence for the Druids, imaginary or, in some cases, invented. From S. R. Meyrick and C. H. Smith's **The Costume of the Original Inhabitants of the British Isles.**

*M*istletoe: a plant which was believed
to have magical properties. Pliny
described how the plant was collected in
special ceremonies, and how it was used
in healing.

In the Renaissance the writings of the
ancient Greeks and Romans became increasingly well known. Men such as Julius Caesar
and Pliny described the Druids, stating that
they were found in Britain and Gaul (broadly
speaking modern France) and that, amongst
other things, they were priests. Julius Caesar
mentions human sacrifice, while Pliny
describes them as worshipping in woodland
groves and collecting mistletoe.

Making the Past

During the Renaissance it was increasingly
realized that some features in the landscape,
for example what we now recognize as prehis-
toric burial mounds, had been made by
ancient peoples. With the 'discovery' of so-
called 'primitive' peoples or 'savages' in the
Americas, this gave the Renaissance thinkers
intellectual and concrete materials to create an
image of antiquity.

Modern scholarship distinguishes carefully
between different sorts of evidence, but in the

Renaissance the idea of the past was something novel, and people envisaged the past as an unchanging time either before or after the biblical Deluge. In this timeless past the different sorts of evidence could happily co-exist. The challenge for the later, Enlightenment, thinkers was to relate this past to the modern world. Mostly this was done by creating myths which related peoples, usually nations, to Noah and the Garden of Eden.

With the knowledge at his disposal Aylett Sammes's 1676 depiction of the Druids involvement in human sacrifice is just what might be expected. In a similar vein John Aubrey (1626–97) wrote:

> *Let us imagine what kind of a countrie this was in the time of the ancient Britons . . . a shady dismal wood: and the inhabitants almost as savage as the beasts whose skins were their only raiment. The language British . . . Their religion is at large described by Caesar. Their priests were Druids. Some of their temples I pretend to have restor'd, as Avebury, Stonehenge &c. . . They were two or three degrees, I suppose, less savage than the Americans.*

These were serious attempts to build a past with the intellectual and physical materials available. Yet in Britain, at least, this was to change. After the making of this past in the Renaissance and Enlightenment, the next 200 years saw little advance in the materials available to understand it. It was, however, increasingly accepted that the ancient Britons spoke a Celtic language, allowing them to be linked with the ancient Gauls, fellow Celtic speakers.

Ironically much of this stagnation stemmed from the use made by William Stukeley (1687–1765) of Aubrey's unpublished work. Stukeley elaborated upon

The Wicker Image: Aylett Sammes's 1676 interpretation of Julius Caesar's description of Gaulish sacrifice by filling enormous wickerwork images with men and then setting them alight. From Britannia Antiqua Illustrata.

The Wicker Image.

the idea of Druids and stone circles, and, setting his work in the context of current theological debate, saw them as purveyors of natural religion, a form of pre-Christian Christianity.

Stukeley's work set the scene for the extravagances of romanticism. Druids, now portrayed as philosophers and priests instead of 'savages', symbolized mysticism and were often viewed with nationalistic pride. For example in Meyrick and Smith's 1815 acquatint the grove and the white gown are icons for the Roman texts, the (shrouded) altar and some of the ornaments are icons for antiquities, but the savages of ethnography have been replaced by a philosopher. An increased awareness of the heroic world of the early Irish tales in which Druids are mentioned provided the finishing touches.

Aubrey had attempted to understand the past as it might have been. Stukeley and others conjured up the origins of many of the modern images of Druids: of Druids as imagined.

The Classical Writers

Ultimately all these British attempts to illustrate the Druids drew on the writings and philosophies of the Greek and Romans. Those works do not survive in their original form, but as copies of copies. Julius Caesar's *Battle for Gaul*,

A silver denarius coin issued by Julius Caesar which commemorates his victory in Gaul. Behind the defeated Gaul is a triumphal display of Gaulish weapons, including a war trumpet or carnyx.

A gold stater coin of the Aulerci Eburovices, a tribe who lived in Normandy. Just below the ear of the stylized face is a representation of a boar.

which gives the fullest account of the Druids, was written in the 1st century BC, but the oldest surviving version is almost a thousand years later.

These ancient sources are not insiders' views of the Druids or of Celtic societies, but those of foreigners. The act of defining the differences between peoples helps to reinforce what is unique to the people making the definitions,

so the Roman writers tell us as much about how they understood their own Roman world as it does about the other peoples. As the classical world did not have a priesthood comparable to the Druids, they were often mentioned by classical writers because they were different.

Most ancient writers described the Celtic society of the time of the dramatic expansion of the Roman Empire by the conquest of western Europe from the 2nd century BC onwards. Before conquest there was often extensive contact, diplomatic and commercial, between the classical and 'barbarian' (simply meaning non-Greek speaking) worlds; such contact could already have caused changes in the barbarian societies described by the writers.

' The dying Gaul', a Roman copy of a Greek statue which formed part of a group commemorating the defeat of Celtic invaders by King Attalus I in 232 BC. The statues were sited in the temple of Athena Nikephoros at Pergamon in modern Turkey.

The Roman authors also wrote within particular literary genres. Thus Julius Caesar's descriptions of the customs of the Britons and Gauls are in a format well-known from other enthographic descriptions and are found half-way through *The Battle for Gaul*, indicating the importance he attached to them. Even so, we are not told the conventions used in translating Celtic ideas and words into Latin.

The earliest references to Druids are from the early 2nd century BC, and most date to the 2nd and 1st centuries BC. A smaller number come from the 1st century AD and mention the suppression of the Druids by Roman emperors, with a few rhetorical references in the 4th century to magicians. Most references are to Gaul, and because many classical writers copied earlier works it has often been assumed that differences between authors were due to mistakes in copying. However, it is more likely that the differences are due to changes in Celtic society and the roles of Druids over 300 years, and to local or regional

11

differences: the lst century AD writers described a situation where Gaul had been under Roman authority for a century. Allowing for this, the classical authors give a generally consistent account of a group of religious specialists, who were effectively a priesthood.

Julius Caesar described the 'only two classes of men of any account or importance' in Gaulish society as the *equites* (nobles) and the *Druidae*, or Druids. Below them in social status were the unfree *plebs* who generally did not own land. Caesar outlines three main roles for the Druids: they were in charge of religion, judges and arbitrators in disputes and teachers and keepers of knowledge.

'*The Gauls claim that they are all descended from Father Dis; they say this is the tradition handed down to them by the Druids. For this reason they reckon periods of time, not in days but in nights...they go on the principle that night comes first and is followed by day*' (*Julius Caesar*, **Battle for Gaul**, *VI, 18*).

Earlier writers also referred to *Bards* (described as poets) and *Vates* (responsible for sacrifices and divination). As described by Caesar the Druids also oversaw sacrifice and divination, so it may be that when he wrote they had assumed sole responsibility for this. Sacrifice and divination, the prediction of the future from the death-throes or entrails of the sacrificed, whether animal or human, was clearly an important role for the Druids.

Caesar translated the names of some of the Gods of the Gauls into Latin – Mercury (the god worshipped most), Apollo, Mars, Jupiter, and Minerva are named – but this tells us little of how the Gauls thought of them. He did, however, describe some beliefs:

The Druids attach particular importance to the belief that the soul does not perish but passes after death from one body to another . . . They hold long discussions about the heavenly bodies and their movements, about the size of the universe and the earth, about the nature of the physical world, and about the power and properties of the immortal gods. (Battle for Gaul VI, 14)

He also stated that the Druids were widely respected and powerful, and exempted from military service and taxation. Although they were literate, they did not write their teachings down, and he supposed that this was because they did not want their doctrines to be accessible to the ordinary people. Restricting access to their knowledge, which was vital at sacrifices and religious ceremonies, as well as to their roles as arbitrators and administrators of justice, would maintain their important position.

The descriptions of Druids sacrificing animals in groves and acting as healers appear later, after the attempts to suppress the Druids, in the works of such

A **contemporary marble portrait bust of Julius Caesar (100–44 BC). His Commentaries on his own conquest of Gaul provide the longest account, as well as a first-hand one, of the Druids.**

1st-century AD writers as Pliny and Mela. These suppressions may have been as much an attempt to curb the power of the Druids as keepers of knowledge and prophesy, and as arbitrators of justice, as acts of religious intolerance.

Gaul had been under Roman rule for a century by the time that Pliny speculated that the name Druid came from the Greek for oak-tree, *drus*, and wrote:

Druids – Gallic magicians – hold nothing more sacred than mistletoe and the oak tree. They choose oak groves for the sake of the tree, and never perform rites except in the presence of a branch of it. Mistletoe is gathered preferably on the sixth day of the moon. Having feasted beneath the trees they bring forward two white bulls. A sacerdos *in a white robe cuts the mistletoe with a golden sickle, and it is caught in a white cloak. The bulls are then killed. Mistletoe is known as all 'healing'. It is believed to impart fecundity to barren animals, and is used as an antidote to all poisons.*

(Natural History, XVI, 249)

Archaeological Evidence

The romantic association of Druids and stone circles and Pliny's account of the sacred grove has suggested to many that Celtic religion was practised in the open air, in natural places. Until very recently it was thought that this would have left few, if any, traces. The building of the rare temple sites like Roquepertuse in southern France, with religious statues and human skulls set in niches,

A reconstruction of part of the façade of the Roquepertuse temple. Human skulls were placed in the niches and the whole structure, which was painted, closed off an overhang in a low cliff to define the temple. The site lay in an **oppidum** *or* **town-like settlement.**

17

```
XIIII          IVOS        • XIIII III    IVODIBCAN
XXV    •  D AMB IVOS              DIVERTOMV
  M EQVOS ANMM...            M SAMON MAT

I          D      IVOS        I         N   DVMANIVO
II      PRINI LAGVOS          II  III D       IVOS
III  M  D  SIMIVOS            III III D        DVM
IIII    D      IVOS           IIII  M  D        AMB
V       D D    AMB            V        D
VI   M  D      AMB            VI   M   D   PRIN IOVDIN
VII     D  SIMIVISO           VII              DVM
VIII    D  ELEMBI             VIII
VIIII   D  ELEMBI             VIIII IIIMD
XI      D  ELEMBI             X    M   D
        D      AMB            XI       D       AMB
        D                     XII  M   D
III  M  D  SEMIVIS            XIII IIIMD
XIIII M D  SEMIVIS            XIIII IIIMD
  V  M  D  SEMICANO           XV   IIIMD

ATENOVX                       ATENOVX
I   M   D  SEMIVIS            I         D     DVMAN
II  M   D  SEMIVIS            II  III   D  TRINVXSAM
III •   D  AMBSIMIVIS         III       D       AMB
IIII    D                     IIII III M D
V   III D      AMB            V    III  D       AMB
VI  III D  SIMISO             VI   IIIMD        AMB
VII III D  ELIMAMB            VII  IIIMD  INIS  R
VIII III D ELEMB              VIII      N  INIS R
VIIII    D AMBELEM            VIIII     N  INIS R
X                            X    IIIMD
XI  III D      AMB            XI  III  D  AMB IVOS
XII III D                     XII IIIMD      IVOS
III III D      AMB            XIII     D  AMB IVOS
XIII III D                    XIIII M  D      IVOS
XIIII   D                     XV       D  AMBIVOS
XV      D      AMB

M ELEMBAN                     M DVMAN ANM
        D                     I   SAMON PRIOVDIXIV
I                             II        N      IVOS
                              III       D      IVOS
                              IIII      D      IVOS
                                   PRINNI LAGET
                                        N  INIS  R
```

could be accounted for by the long Greek and Roman contacts with the Mediterranean coast of Gaul. Indeed, some of the sites were dated to after the Roman conquest of the region late in the 2nd century BC, the same time as some of the references to Druids.

A little archaeological evidence supports the accounts of the classical writers. The 3rd century AD Coligny calendar, probably from a temple, was written in Gaulish which was by then an ancient language, and not Latin. It shows that time was counted in months which were lucky or unlucky. Each month was divided in two by the word ATEN-OVX, when the waxing moon wanes. A few objects might be associated with Druids. Some rare short swords, so small that they are really symbolic swords, were inlaid with golden symbols which seem to represent the phases of moon. The swords may have been used in sacrifice and divination. Pairs of 'spoons' may also have been used in such rituals, but apart from this scant evidence can anything more be said?

T he remains of the Coligny calendar. By placing pegs in the small holes next to each day it is eventually possible to reconcile the lunar and solar years. Each month is divided into lucky and unlucky halves by the word atenox.

A n anthropomorphic hilted short sword from Mainz. This tiny sword (length 450 mm) was a symbolic weapon, perhaps used in sacrifices. Just below the hilt are a circle and crescent both inlaid with gold, separated by a vertical line. Other finds show that these symbols probably represent the different phases of the moon.

19

A pair of ritual 'spoons' from Ireland. The bowl of one 'spoon' from each pair is always marked by a cross, the bowl of the other always has a small hole. Were they used for divination?

Archaeological evidence allows us to assess the Druids or religious specialists, and Iron Age religion more generally, in different ways. Unlike the historical texts, the evidence continues to increase.

As many Greek and Roman writers referred to central and western Europe as being inhabited by Celts or Gauls (sometimes using the words synonymously), it seems that the Greeks and Romans recognized a broad group of peoples comparable to the German peoples or the Iberians. It is likely that many of these peoples spoke Celtic languages, but it cannot be assumed that the distribution of those modern languages called Celtic, many not recorded until the 18th and 19th centuries, is the same as their ancient distribution, or that this did not change in the intervening 2,000 years.

None the less, archaeologists were quick to link the archaeological evidence with that of the classical writers who also mentioned Celtic migrations and the linguistic evidence, using it as an index of Celtic ethnicity to illustrate them. At a broad level this may be correct but it has frequently limited archaeological interpretation to description, obscuring the many differences within the Celtic world.

For example, some religious practices were followed over large areas. The offering of hoards of gold torques and coins to the gods is found from Britain to the Czech Republic, but the types of torques, coins, and the sort of place

*T*he Niederzier hoard of torques and coins was found in a settlement, buried next to a post which may have been a cult idol.

OVERLEAF

*G*old torques from Needwood Forest (top left), Ipswich and Snettisham. The Great Torque from Snettisham (bottom right) is the finest of the 75 more or less complete torques and fragments of 100 more, nearly all of gold but with some of silver, found in the 12 or more hoards known from the site.

*T*hird-century BC Britons, based on evidence from East Yorkshire. The man's body decoration, which is hypothetical, copies the decoration on a sword scabbard. Painting by Peter Connolly.

*A*n artist's interpretation of a 1st century BC cremation at Westhampnett, West Sussex. Shrines, pyres and burials suggested here to be marked by wooden figurines, were all found at this religious site. Painting by Julian Cross.

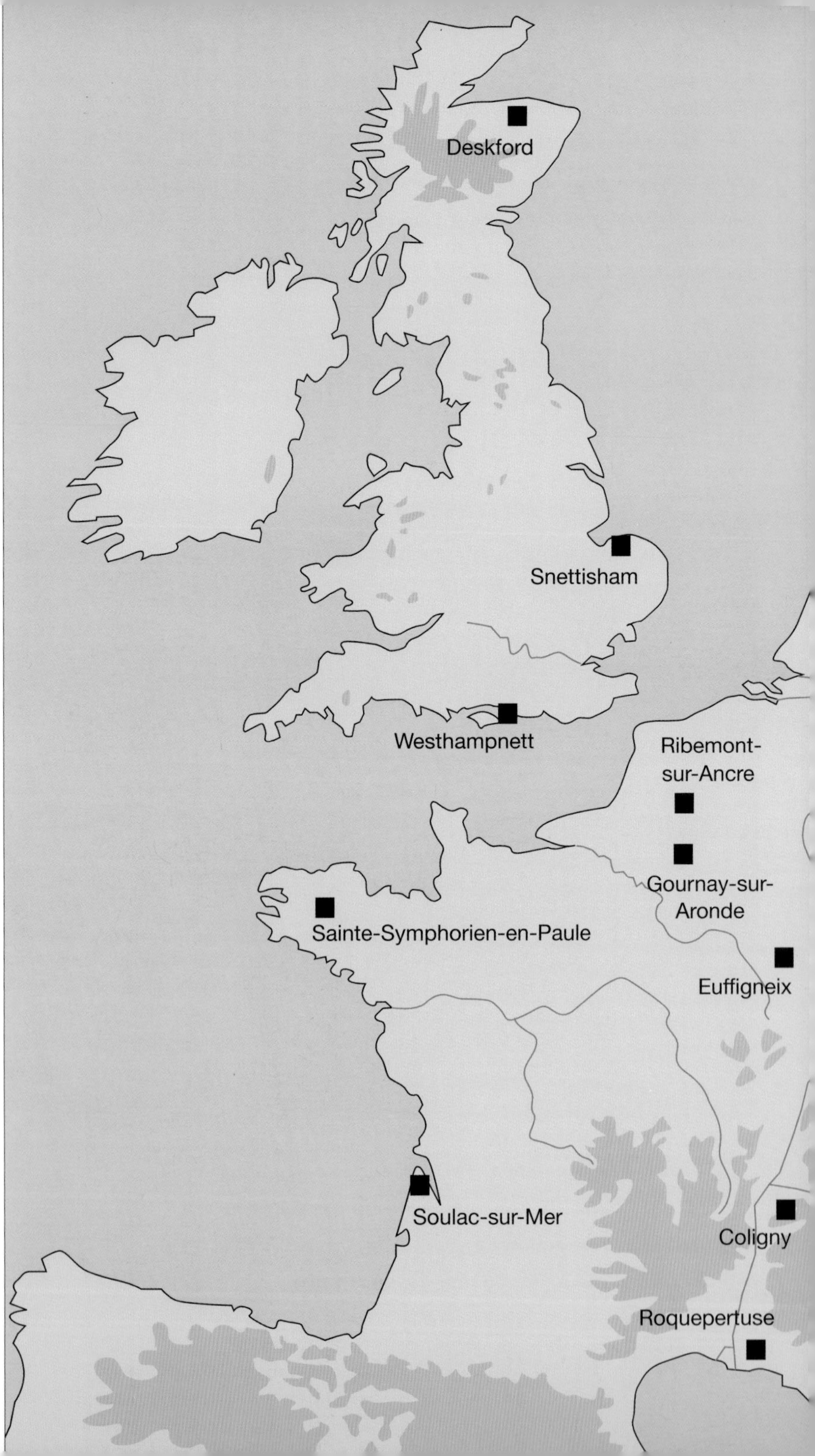

Deskford

Snettisham

Westhampnett

Ribemont-
sur-Ancre

Gournay-sur-
Aronde

Sainte-Symphorien-en-Paule

Euffigneix

Soulac-sur-Mer

Coligny

Roquepertuse

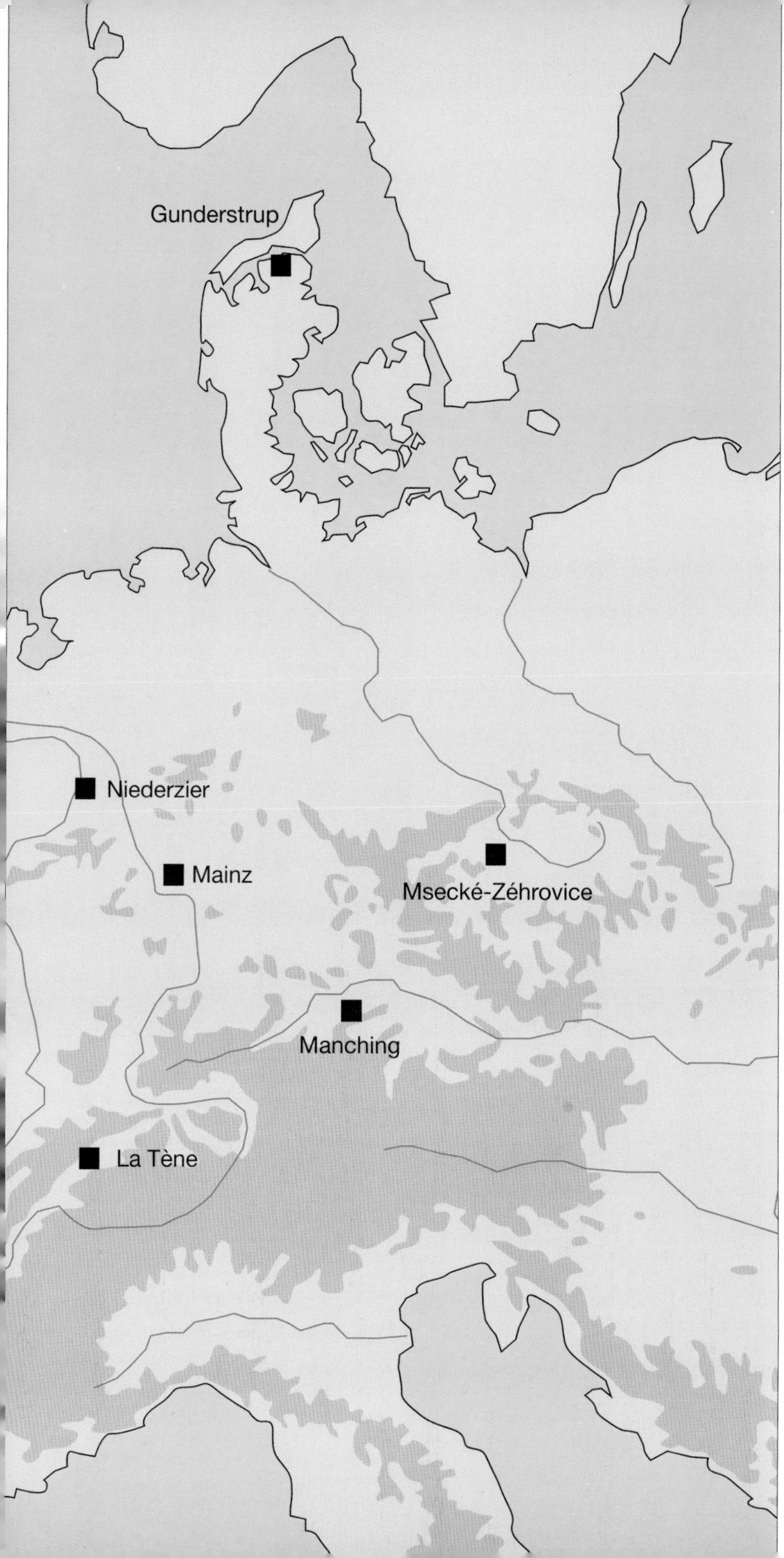

Gunderstrup

Map showing sites mentioned in the text.

Niederzier

Mainz

Msecké-Zéhrovice

Manching

La Tène

where the offering was made is nearly always different. A sword sheath decorated with 'Celtic "art"', an art imbued with religious symbolism, might be found over much of continental Europe but the details of a find from Yorkshire declare it to be British. The man with whom it was buried, and his partner, will have lived in round houses. In continental Europe, houses were rectangular but on some settlements in Britain temples or shrines are distinguished by being square. In the 2nd and 1st centuries BC cremation burial was practised over much of Europe, but the exact rites differed from region to region. In other regions inhumation burial, or ways of disposing of the dead which did not require burial were still practised.

Later Iron Age Rituals

This diversity is also seen in the evidence for Celtic religious practises in the 2nd and 1st centuries BC. This is late in the period commonly called the La Tène Iron Age after the finds made at the site of La Tène in Switzerland. Most of this evidence comes from votive deposits, sacri-

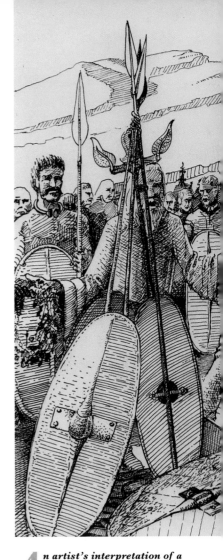

*A*n artist's interpretation of a sacrifice taking place under the supervision of a Druid at La Tène with Lake Neuchâtel and the Jura Mountains in the background. The details are based on finds from Switzerland. Drawing by André Rapin.

fices made to the gods to obtain their support or to thank them for it. Only rarely is it possible to determine what sort of god, such as of fertility or warfare, to whom the offerings were made. The gods may have had many faces or atttributes.

At the site of La Tène itself a number of bridges or jetties projected into a tributary of Lake Neuchâtel. From the 3rd to 1st centuries BC weapons, particularly swords and spears, often deliberately hacked and broken, were thrown into the water. Finds of human remains suggest that people were also sacrificed. Many of the finds from this site are weapons and the placing of weaponry, much of which bears the finest 'Celtic "art"' known, in rivers or bogs is well known. The boar in particular seems to have been associated with warfare and display. The towering, boar-headed war trumpet or *carnyx* from Deskford was probably made early in the Roman period, but it is a well-known Late Iron Age type and it was deliberately buried in a bog. The boar from Soulac-sur-Mer was found on a beach. Originally decorating a battle standard, the boar had been ritually destroyed, the pieces rolled-up, and then buried.

These offerings to water may have been to goddesses, but whomever gifted them, there is no immediately obvious female partner to these masculine offerings. While it is possible to infer some of the rituals at sites such as La Tène, evidence for the beliefs which demanded them is elusive. A tantalizing image of what may have existed is given by the myth(s) depicted on the Gundestrup cauldron. In the late 2nd century BC this silver cauldron was dismantled and buried in a bog in Jutland, an area generally inhabited by Germanic peoples. As the cauldron was made in south-eastern Europe, there is little doubt that both the makers and users of the cauldron knew some Celtic beliefs, but the mythology it depicts, replete with elephants, may well not be Celtic.

A modern reconstruction of the Deskford carnyx or war trumpet. This towering, boar-headed object had a range of several octaves and a wooden tongue in the mouth which could be played percussively.

Despite the legacy of romanticism, rivers, bogs and other 'natural' places were not the only places venerated as cult sites. In the great *oppidum* (a settlement like a town) of Manching, several shrines or temples are known, either small square or round buildings. However, a miniature tree, of wood and bronze clad in gold leaf and surely a cult idol, was buried in a pit in the settlement, not in the shrines. The small statue with a torque and lyre found at

OVERLEAF

The Gundestrup cauldron, found by peat-cutters in Denmark 1891, was probably made in Thrace (modern Bulgaria) 2,000 years earlier, perhaps for an invading Celtic tribe. The complex iconography draws on many traditions, some from as far away as India.

The miniature cult tree from Manching (height 700 mm). Made from wood, the tree, which is complete with berries, was sheathed in bronze and adorned with leaves of gold. Placed on a golden tray, it was buried as an offering to the gods.

Saint-Symphorien-en-Paule, representing a bard or, more likely, a god was also found in a settlement. It is a rare example of Late Iron Age sculpture but it also suggests that in daily life there was not a clear distinction between the sacred and the profane, and it may be here, in the home, that the seemingly absent female counterpart to the masculine offerings in 'natural' places might be found.

Although a number of statues of gods have been found in Gaul, such as the one from Euffigneix, most are likely to date to the Roman period when sacred images were required in religious ceremonies. In many cases the style of representation, even the very idea of a physical image or idol was new. As such they are a Roman rather than Celtic way of seeing and talking about religion.

We have seen that Iron Age temples were once assumed to be rare throughout the Celtic world, yet an increasing number of Late Iron Age examples are now known. Numerous four-sided compounds, or *Viereck-shanzen*, have been found in southern Germany and the Czech Republic. Some are likely to be farms, but others have shrines or temples in one corner, and deep wells which might have served as ritual shafts. The

*R*econstruction of the boar-shaped battle standard found broken and rolled up in pieces, presumably as a votive offering, on the beach at Soulac-sur-Mer.

*S*tatue of a god, of Gallo-Roman date, from Euffigneix. The god wears a torque and is adorned with a boar and a (probably) human eye. Representations of gods were rare in Gaul until the Roman period.

A n artist's impression of a **Viereckshanze**, set against a background of earlier burial mounds. Some of these enclosures had small temples in one corner, and wells or shafts which could have been used for ritual purposes. Other enclosures of this type may have been farms.

T he stone head of a god wearing a torque from Mšecké Žéhrovice, another rare example of Celtic sculpture.

famous stone head of a god, again wearing a torque, was buried, perhaps after being deliberately broken, just outside the *Viereckschanze* at Mšecké Zéhrovice.

The most important new evidence for Late Iron Age religion has come from northern France, where Roman temples were often built on the sites of Iron Age shrines. At these shrines the definition of a sacred space by a ditch may have been more important than a house or temple for the god. Underneath the Roman temple at Ribemont-sur-Ancre Iron Age ditches enclosed a square

37

compound. In at least two corners of which long bones, mainly of people, intermingled with weapons, were carefully stacked around a post. Nearby were the remains of headless human torsos, which may have been displayed around the edge of the compound.

At Gournay-sur-Aronde, the first Iron Age structures were aligned on the cardinal points of the (modern) compass and later on a temple was built on this alignment. The brilliant excavation and analyses of this site have shown how animal sacrifices were placed in a pit in the centre of the enclosure before their remains were carefully laid in specified places of the boundary ditch. The human remains also appear to have been dismembered, in much the same way as the numerous finds of weapons. The reconstruction of the Iron Age temple suggested by the excavators is very similar to the types found later on in Roman Gaul. The sorts and methods of sacrifices and the precise, symbolic, use of space at Gournay-sur-Aronde reveal the site as a microcosm. It lays bare, and is a symbol for, the ways in which the ancient Gauls tried to understand their world.

The existence of cult sites such as La Tène and temples such as Gournay-sur-Aronde with their evidence for repeated rituals involving the sacrifice of people, animals and worldly goods, suggests that these sites served communities and that religious specialists may have been in charge of them. In this respect the archaeological evidence and the testimonies of the classical writers complement each other. As well as feeding the gods, one of most important roles of blood sacrifice is divination; determining when is a good or bad time to do things. This also requires the making and marking of time, and a traditional knowledge through which to interpret the omens.

Such then is the image which emerges of the ancient Druids. Romanticism,

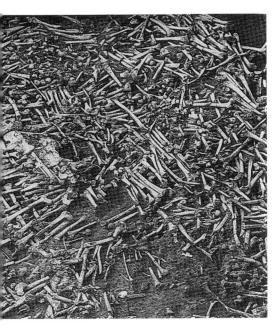

*O*ne of the two ossuaries so far known, at *Ribemont-sur-Ancre*. Made *from human long bones, the* ossuary was built around a post. It seems likely that the torsos of the dead were displayed, along with weapons, around the boundary of the temple site.

whether ancient, modern, or New Age, has treated the Druids in the same ways as mysterious, mystic, noble and other worldly. Always as different, as 'other'. Yet they were also trying to understand their own world, their gods and their own futures. That world was very different, and it was not romantic.

*T*he placement of human and animal remains in the enclosing ditch at Gournay-sur-Aronde. Deposits of weapons were also carefully placed in the ditch. Drawing after Jean-Louis Brunaux.

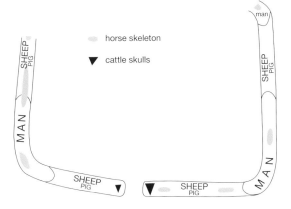

horse skeleton

▼ cattle skulls

39

PHOTOGRAPHIC ACKNOWLEDGEMENTS
Cover National Museum, Prague; p. 3 e.t. archive;
pp. 4–5 Zefa; p. 7 Fortean Picture Library;
pp. 8, 9 Weidenfeld & Nicolson Archives;
pp. 10–11 Archivio Fotografico dei Musei
Capitolini, Rome; pp. 12–13 Zefa; p. 15 AKG
London/National Museum of Archaeology,
Naples; pp. 16–17 Prähistorische Staatssammlung
Museum für Vor-und Frügeschichte, Munich;
p. 18 Photo Ch. Thioc, Musée de la Civilisation
Gallo-Romaine, Lyon; p. 19 Landmuseum, Mainz;
p. 20 National Museum of Ireland, Dublin;
p. 21 Rheinisches Landesmuseum, Bonn. Photo
H. Lilenthal; pp. 23–3 AKG London;
p. 24 Peter Connolly; p. 25 Julian Cross and Wessex
Archaeology; pp. 28–9 Verlag Neue Zurcher
Zeitung, Zurich; pp. 31, 32 © The Trustees of the
National Museums of Scotland 1997;
pp. 33–4 The National Museum, Copenhagen;
p. 34 Prähistorisches Staatssammlung Museum für
Vor-und Frügeschichte, Munich;
p. 35t Romisch-Germanisches Zentralmuseum,
Forchunginstitut für Vor-und Frügeschichte, Mainz;
p. 35b St-Germain-en-Laye, Musée des Antiquités
Nationales © RMN – Jean Schormans;
p. 36 Konrad Theiss Verlag, Stuttgart;
p. 37 National Museum Prague;
p. 39 Jean-Louis Brunaux.

First published in Great Britain 1997
by George Weidenfeld and Nicolson Ltd
The Orion Publishing Group
5 Upper St Martin's Lane
London WC2H 9EA

A CIP catalogue record for this book is available
from the British Library
ISBN 0 297 823191

Picture Research: Suzanne Williams

Designed by Harry Green

Typeset in Baskerville